What Every CATECHIST SHOULD KNOW

What Every CATECHIST SHOULD KNOW

Joseph D. White, Ph.D.

Our Sunday Visitor Publishing Division
Our Sunday Visitor, Inc.
Huntington, Indiana 46750

Nihil Obstat:
Rev. Kevin Rai
Imprimatur:
✠ Gregory Aymond
Bishop of Austin
January 2, 2003

The Scripture citations used in this work are taken from the Catholic Edition of the *Revised Standard Version of the Bible* (RSV), copyright © 1965 and 1966 by the Division of Christian Education of the National Council of the Churches of Christ in the United States of America. Used by permission. All rights reserved.

Excerpts from the English translation of the *Catechism of the Catholic Church, Second Edition*, for use in the United States of America, copyright © 1994 and 1997, United States Catholic Conference — Libreria Editrice Vaticana. Used by permission. All rights reserved.

Excerpts from the English translation of the *General Directory for Catechesis*, copyright © 1997 by Libreria Editrice Vaticana, used with permission.

Excerpts from English translations of *Gaudium et Spes, Dei Verbum, Lumen Gentium, Sacram unctionem infirmorum*, and *Ad Gentes* from the Vatican website, *www.vatican.va*.

Every reasonable effort has been made to determine copyright holders of excerpted materials and to secure permissions as needed. If any copyrighted materials have been inadvertently used in this work without proper credit being given in one form or another, please notify Our Sunday Visitor in writing so that future printings of this work may be corrected accordingly.

Copyright © 2003 by Our Sunday Visitor Publishing Division, Our Sunday Visitor, Inc. All rights reserved.

With the exception of short excerpts for critical reviews, no part of this work may be reproduced or transmitted in any form or by any means whatsoever without permission in writing from the publisher. Write:
Our Sunday Visitor Publishing Division
Our Sunday Visitor, Inc.
200 Noll Plaza
Huntington, IN 46750

ISBN: 1-931709-70-X (Inventory No. R34)

Cover and interior design by Monica Haneline
Interior photos from OSV files and Comstock, Inc.
Cover photo from Comstock, Inc.

PRINTED IN THE UNITED STATES OF AMERICA

Acknowledgments

Thanks to my wife, Ana, for hanging in there with me when I spend late nights on these projects.

Thanks to Charlene O'Connell and the staff of the catechetical office of the Diocese of Austin for your support and insights.

To all at Our Sunday Visitor — you guys are great! Thanks for another wonderful opportunity.

This book is dedicated to my mother, father, and grandparents, who first taught me about God and his Word, and is written in memory of Msgr. Charles Kelly, who taught this "cradle Protestant" so much about the treasures of the Catholic faith.

About the Author

Joseph D. White, Ph.D., is the director of faith formation at St. Thomas Aquinas Parish in College Station, Texas.

He provides additional resources for catechists at www.catechistsonline.com

Contents

Introduction 8

First Task of Catechesis 10
   We Believe: Promoting Knowledge of the Faith

   Part One: Who Is God, and
How Can We Know Him? 10

   Part Two: Sin, Grace, and Redemption 17

   Part Three: The Church, the Saints, and Mary,
Our Mother 23

Second Task of Catechesis 30
   We Celebrate: Liturgical Education

   Part One: Sacraments of Initiation 30

   Part Two: Sacraments of Healing 36

   Part Three: Sacraments at the Service
of Communion 42

Third Task of Catechesis 48
   We Love: Moral Formation

Fourth Task of Catechesis 55
   We Pray: Conversation with God

Fifth Task of Catechesis 60
   We Are One in Christ: Education for Community Life

Sixth Task of Catechesis 65
   We Are Sent: Missionary Initiation

Endnotes 71

Introduction

As a director of faith formation, I frequently speak with members of the parish who would like to work as catechists, but feel somewhat intimidated and wonder whether they know enough to teach the Catholic faith to others. Many of these individuals know more than they think they do; many are "cradle Catholics" who know a great deal about Catholic teaching through their own experiences in parish life or Catholic school. Still, they are searching for a way to consolidate and organize that knowledge so that it will be conducive to the tasks of catechesis.

This book is designed as a catechist-specific primer on the basics of the Catholic faith. It organizes essential doctrines according to the six tasks of catechesis mentioned in the *General Directory for Catechesis*. Each chapter begins with reflection questions that draw from the catechist's own experience, then offers some basic points from Scripture and the *Catechism of the Catholic Church*. Chapters conclude with some ideas for sharing each concept with children and a list of references from Scripture and the *Catechism* for further study. The book can be used as a tool for catechist formation sessions or in personal study by the catechist.

The depth and richness of our faith make it difficult to offer such a brief summary. This guide is intended to be a beginning for those who want to "brush up" on their Church doctrine, as well as an organizing tool for catechists who seek more ways to share their faith with children. It is not meant to replace the *Catechism*, which offers a much more comprehensive overview of the basic teachings of the Church.

God bless you as you seek to deepen your own faith and to share it with others.

— THE AUTHOR

I.
First Task of Catechesis

We Believe: Promoting Knowledge of the Faith

Part One: Who Is God, and How Can We Know Him?

"Knowledge of the faith (fides quae) is required by adherence to the faith (fides qua). ... Catechesis must, therefore, lead to "the gradual grasping of the whole truth about the divine plan."

GENERAL DIRECTORY FOR CATECHESIS, 85

For the Catechist / Questions for Reflection

• Who is God to me? What words come to mind when I think of God?

_____

_____

• In what places have I looked for God?

_____

_____

- Where have I been most successful in finding God?

  _____

  _____

Finding God: Sources of Revelation

The *Catechism of the Catholic Church* begins with a discussion of the nature of God and the human desire to know him. This is fitting, for in our discovery of God we find the answers to our most burning human questions: Who am I? Why am I here? What is the meaning of life?

Perhaps the best way to begin answering these questions is to say that we are, in our very essence, an expression of God's love. Out of love he created us, and out of love he reveals himself to us. It makes sense, then, that we should search for and desire to know God. We are by nature religious beings,[1] and we cannot truly know ourselves until we come to know him who created us. "Without the Creator, the creature would disappear."[2]

As Catholic Christians, we believe in one true God. We believe that it is possible to know God through his creation and through his revelation. As beings created in God's image, we are given the light of reason, which we may use to find God. We are also given free will, however, and when pride causes us to focus on ourselves rather than on our Source, our reason is clouded. Because of this, God has chosen to reveal himself to humanity in multiple ways. He has revealed himself gradually, first through his covenants with his people (namely, his promises to Noah, Abraham, and Moses), and most completely in the person of Jesus Christ.

Jesus is the last and definitive Word of God to humanity. He is the "final Word," so we should not expect any further revelation. There is no better way for God to show us who he is than in the person of Jesus. Since the time of Christ, the Gospel has been passed on in two ways — orally (through Sacred Tradition) and in written form (Sacred Scripture).

To preserve the purity of the Gospel message, God gave the Church the gift of apostolic succession. Jesus chose twelve disciples to spread his message. When one disciple, out of his own free will, chose to betray Jesus and later took his own life, the other eleven disciples, under the inspiration of the Holy Spirit, chose another to replace Judas.[3] This tradition has continued to this day, and our contemporary bishops (including the pope) represent an unbroken line of apostolic succession — leaders chosen by Christ — throughout the centuries.

This point is important for a number of reasons. The New Testament as we know it did not exist for the first few hundred years of the life of the Church. There were literally hundreds of manuscripts about Christ and the Church, and some confusion about which were truly the Word of God. In the year 367, Saint Athanasius proposed a definitive list of the books of the New Testament. His list was adopted by Pope Saint Damasus I in 382 and confirmed by a council of Catholic bishops in the year 419. For the next several hundred years, books of Scripture were unavailable to most Christians because the printing press had not yet been invented. All this is to say that a Church built on Scripture alone would have been impossible for many years, and Catholics would argue that such a Church is still impossible. Scripture is interpreted in different ways by sincere people, resulting in thousands of Protestant Christian sects.

This points to the necessity of apostolic succession and Sacred Tradition. The Church relied on Sacred Tradition to guide her through the first centuries of her existence. She relied on the magisterium (the Church's teaching authority, passed down from the apostles to the pope and his fellow bishops) to know which books of Scripture were divinely inspired. We continue to rely on Sacred Tradition and the teaching authority (the magisterium) to interpret Scripture in the modern world. Sacred Tradition is the context in which Scripture arose, and the context in which it must be interpreted.

God's Word is transmitted in an active way. While the Gospel (the "Good News" of Christ) does not change, it is passed on by a living Church in which God plays an active role. We can come to know God today through study of his Word in Sacred Scripture and Sacred Tradition, which "form one sacred deposit of the word of God." [4]

The Holy Trinity

So what do Sacred Scripture and Sacred Tradition tell us about God? One of the most basic principles about God is also one of the most mysterious. Our God is one God in three persons, three in one — Father, Son, and Holy Spirit. This is the doctrine of the Holy Trinity. Saint Patrick used a shamrock to explain the Trinity to his students — three leaves, one shamrock. This is a helpful illustration, but a somewhat incomplete one. Each leaf of the shamrock is only part of the whole, while the Father, Son, and Holy Spirit are all God in his fullness. No earthly analogy can fully explain this divine mystery. The best analogy I have heard was given in a talk by Dr. Michael Corso of Boston College at the annual meeting of the National Conference for Catechetical Leadership. Dr. Corso likened the Trinity to a song, which can be expressed in its entirety as a thought in one's head (when you have a song on your mind, for example), as written sheet music, or as a performance of the song on an instrument or by the human voice. Dr. Corso likened the Holy Spirit to the latter, saying that just as the same song might sound a little different when it is played on different

instruments or performed by different persons, the same Spirit may express himself differently through each of us, given our unique talents and personalities.

God in his fullness has always existed. Neither the Father, nor the Son, nor the Holy Spirit is a created being. God first revealed himself as loving Father, making and keeping promises with his people, giving them what they needed, guiding them through difficult times, and welcoming them back when they had wandered away. The Father showed his love most completely by sending Jesus, his only Son: Jesus who showed us what it meant to live love on earth; Jesus who gave himself up to die to show us the depth of his love; Jesus who was raised from the dead and reigns triumphantly with the Father. Jesus promised the Holy Spirit to his disciples. God would dwell within his people, making their very bodies his temple and empowering them with spiritual gifts.

God — the one God in three persons — is all-powerful, all-seeing, and all-knowing, yet he desires intimacy with each of us. This is perhaps the greatest mystery of all. The same God who created the universe knows your name. He sees your strengths and your weaknesses. He knows what makes you laugh and what makes you cry. He loves you, and wants to be your friend. What an awesome and wonderful thought. What an impossible but necessary blessing!

Read More about It

For more information on the nature of God and how we come to know him, please see the following citations from Scripture and the *Catechism*:

Matthew 3:16-17

Matthew 28:18-19

Mark 12:29

John 1:1-4

John 14:8-14

Catechism of the Catholic Church, Nos. 27-141

Ideas for Teaching Children about the Nature of God

"Three persons in one God" is a concept that is difficult even for adults to grasp. Teaching this doctrine is ideally a gradual process that unfolds as children mature intellectually. Initial instruction on the Trinity (in preschool and kindergarten) may include teaching the "different names of God" and the Sign of the Cross.

For students ages ten and older, use the "song" analogy described earlier to illustrate the Trinity. Make the analogy come to life by inviting a musician to visit the class and play the song.

Students of all ages may benefit from using the traditional symbols of the Trinity (triangles, the shamrock) in an art project. Talk about how the symbols remind us of the "three persons in one God."

Ideas for Teaching Children about Ways We Can Know God

Young children often are not ready to read directly from the Bible, but having the Bible in a prominent place in the classroom (such as on a classroom altar with some statuary and a candle) can highlight the importance of Scripture. Discuss how Scripture is one way God speaks to us. Older children (sixth grade and above) also may be interested in learning how the Bible came to be. It's important for them to know that the Bible was a collection of writings that came from the Church and her Tradition.

Take a walk outside with your class and discuss what you learn about God from the things you see in nature ... the sky reveals that God is very big; the clouds remind us that he provides water and the things we need; the individual blades of grass, the lines in the leaves on trees, and the petals on a flower remind us that God pays attention to very small details.

Part Two: Sin, Grace, and Redemption

"Jesus shows, at the same time, that God, with the coming of his Kingdom, offers the gift of integral salvation, frees from sin, brings one to communion with the Father, grants divine sonship, and in conquering death, promises eternal life."

GENERAL DIRECTORY FOR CATECHESIS, 102

For the Catechist / Questions for Reflection

- When have I acted outside of God's will and caused negative consequences for myself or for others?

- What does salvation mean to me?

- How do I imagine heaven?

Missing the Mark

We are created in God's image to love and serve him. When God created human beings, he had a beautiful plan for each of us to live in accordance with his will and have all the blessings that accompany such a life. Out of his love for us and his desire that we should choose to do right, God gave human beings free will. Scripture tells us the story of Adam and Eve, who allowed themselves to be overcome by pride, a desire to be like God. Their pride brought sin and death into the world, and sin became intertwined with human nature. This flaw, called original sin, was passed on throughout history and inclines us to sin in defiance of our true nature.

While some Christian denominations teach that humans are inherently evil and sin by virtue of their nature, the Catholic Church affirms the goodness of people as created in God's image. People do not sin because they are evil by nature, but because they have allowed their inherent goodness to be corrupted by selfishness, and this corruption has been transmitted throughout all generations.

The word "sin" literally means "to miss the mark." We sin when we choose to miss the great things God has intended for us. This is an important point. No one knows better than the creator how to care for that which is created. When we buy a complex piece of machinery, we attend to the manufacturer's instructions for caring for the machine. In a similar way, God provides instructions out of love and care for us, knowing that we bring damaging consequences upon ourselves when we behave outside his will. The most damaging consequence of our sin is the fact that through sin, we separate ourselves from God, who is the source of all good things.

Redemption

Because of his great love for us, God cannot allow us to remain helpless in a state of separation from him. From the very beginning, he planned to send his Son to redeem the world.[5] In his *Summa Theologica*, Saint Thomas Aquinas writes that God permits evil in the world to allow for a greater good (1, 3, ad 3). The blessings humanity has gained through God's plan of redemption are greater than what was lost when sin entered the world. Through Jesus Christ, we have the opportunity to be not just created beings living in accordance with God's will, but adopted daughters and sons of God — brothers and sisters of Christ himself!

The word redeem means "to buy back," like when we redeem a gift certificate at a store. God "bought us back" through the sacrifice of his only Son, Jesus, who had no sin, but made himself an offering for our sin. God prepared his people for Jesus' sacrifice by instituting the Passover.[6] The lambs used in the Passover sacrifice prefigured Jesus, who would be called the "Lamb of God." God's sacrifice of his Son is a gift to humanity. It's not something we could earn, but as a gift, it must be accepted.

We accept God's gift of redemption through our faith in Jesus Christ. Faith is more than belief. Think of all the many people you know. You believe they exist, but do you have faith in all of them? Certainly not! Faith means not only belief, but also trust — a trust so profound that it leads to obedience. If you are sick and you truly have faith in your doctor, you will trust the doctor and follow his or her instructions. Likewise, if we truly have faith in Jesus as the Son of God, we will follow him. Jesus makes it clear that following him means dying to our own will, a process that begins with our baptism and continues throughout our lives. The Church teaches that true faith is accompanied by good works.[7] Faith without good works is not faith at all. Sometimes this teaching is misunderstood by those outside the Church, who accuse Catholics of thinking they can "earn their way to heaven." On the contrary, we believe "salvation comes from God alone,"[8] but we receive God's gift of grace through an active faith in him.

Last Things: Heaven, Hell, and Purgatory

We don't know much about the afterlife, but our Catholic faith tells us that life doesn't end with our physical death. Baptized Christians have already sacramentally died and been raised up to walk in new life with Christ. This death and rebirth to new life is completed with our physical death, provided we die in God's grace and friendship. We die to live forever with God.[9] Heaven is the place in which one dwells with God and sees God as he really is.

Dying "in God's grace and friendship" means being free from mortal sin, the kind of sin that separates us from God. Individuals are guilty of mortal sin if they intentionally and with full knowledge violate God's law in a serious (or "grave") matter. Grave matters include murder, adultery, theft, bearing false witness, defrauding another, or dishonoring one's parents. Note that the aforementioned sins are not necessarily mortal sins, but they are serious enough to be mortal sins if they are committed with full intention and knowledge. A purposeful turning away from God is a "radical possibility of human freedom."[10] It is important to note that the very definition of mortal sin requires a purposeful rejection of God's will in one's life, and by default, God himself. God does not will that anyone be separated from him, and even mortal sin is forgiven through celebration of the sacrament of reconciliation. However, those who die in a state of rejection of God separate themselves from him forever. This eternal separation from God is called "hell."

Venial sin is any violation of God's law that does not meet the criteria for mortal sin. Venial sin weakens the work of God in our lives. It harms us because it keeps us from being the people God made us to be. God forgives our venial sins, but they do damage to our own souls and to others. If we die in a state of venial sin, we are not ready to be united with God, who is all-good. In addition, venial sins, which have already been forgiven, may continue to damage us because they have led us to have disordered desires that are not compatible with life with God. The Church teaches that those who die in God's friendship but are still in need of purification in order to enter into his presence are sent to purgatory. Purgatory is the purification by fire to which Scripture refers.[11] While it likely will be immensely painful for many to be purified of the things that keep them from God, purgatory is quite distinct from hell, because it purifies the soul. This purification is a positive, albeit painful, process.

Ideas for Teaching Children about Sin, Grace, and Redemption

Children's understanding of the concept of sin is very limited until about age seven, when their thinking becomes more rule-based and logical. For this reason, most catechetical texts wait until second grade to introduce the concept of sin as a component of preparing children for the sacrament of reconciliation. Distinctions between mortal and venial sin are typically not discussed at this time, however, because children this age have great difficulty understanding this distinction and are very unlikely to commit mortal sin. It is better to introduce this latter concept when children are in middle school and presumably capable of more abstract thought.

Young children (preschool and elementary age) are sometimes easily frightened by discussions of hell, or even purgatory, but they are delighted to imagine what heaven must be like. Ask the children to draw pictures or write about what they imagine heaven to be like. You may wish to arrange their work on a bulletin board somewhere in the classroom.

The paschal mystery is central to the theme of sin, grace, and redemption. Children in fourth grade and above may enjoy exploring the concept of Jesus as our Paschal Lamb by celebrating the Seder (traditional Passover meal) and discussing how the lessons of Passover relate to the death and resurrection of Jesus.

Read More about It

For more information on sin, grace, and redemption, please see the following citations from Scripture and the *Catechism:*

Matthew 7:21

Matthew 19:16-19

Romans 1:16-3:31

Philippians 3:20-21

Revelation 14:10-13, 21:1-22:5

Catechism of the Catholic Church, 161-169; 1010-1037; 1852-1869

Part Three: The Church, the Saints, and Mary, Our Mother

"Hence, when catechesis transmits the mystery of Christ, the faith of the whole people of God echoes in its message throughout the course of history: the faith received by the Apostles from Christ himself and under the action of the Holy Spirit; that of the martyrs who have borne witness to it and still bear witness to it by their blood; that of the saints who have lived it and live it profoundly."

GENERAL DIRECTORY FOR CATECHESIS, 105

"The Blessed Virgin Mary lived these dimensions of faith in the most perfect way. The Church 'venerates in Mary the purest realization of faith.'"

GENERAL DIRECTORY FOR CATECHESIS, 55

For the Catechist / Questions for Reflection

- What makes the Catholic Church different from other institutions?

- What are some traditions or heirlooms that connect me with family members who came before me?

- What words or images come to mind when I hear the word "mother"?

The Catholic Church: Not Just an Institution

With a two-thousand-year history and about one billion members worldwide, the Catholic Church is the largest and longest-lasting institution in human history. In the Nicene Creed we profess "one, holy, catholic, and apostolic Church." This statement is commonly called the "four marks of the Church." Under the authority of Christ, the leadership of the pope and his fellow bishops, and the common faith we profess, we are all part of one body.[12] God bestows holiness on his Church through the sacraments, which sanctify, strengthen, and renew us to perform Christ's work in the world. The Church is "catholic," which literally means "universal," "for everyone," or "containing the whole." The Holy Spirit guides the Church to truth through the gift of apostolic succession. The Church is not merely an institution, but also a mystery. She is a sacrament, a sign of Christ to her members and to the world.

The Communion of Saints

In a certain sense, "the Church" and the "communion of saints" are one and the same.[13] For the Church is the people of God, both the living and those who have died in Christ. The "oneness" of the Church is so powerful that even time and death do not separate its members. We are forever united to those who have come before us and those who will come after us in the faith. In the Dogmatic Constitution of the Church, *Lumen Gentium*, the Second Vatican Council described how living and deceased members of the Church are separated, yet united:

> "At the present time some of his disciples are pilgrims on earth. Others have died and are being purified, while still others are in glory, contemplating 'in full light, God himself triune and one, exactly as he is.' All of us, however, in varying degrees and in different ways share in the same charity toward God and our neighbors, and we all sing the one hymn of glory to our God. All, indeed, who are of Christ and who have his Spirit form one Church and in Christ cleave together."[14]

According to the *Catechism*, our brothers and sisters who have died and are now united more closely with Christ offer prayers for us to the Father.[15] While we can certainly approach God directly, it also makes sense to offer prayers to the saints because they are able to see things from a perspective that is free from selfish interests and material concerns. "The prayer of a righteous man has great power in its effects."[16]

Mary, Our Mother

Mary, the Mother of God, is honored above all other saints. This is consistent with her foretelling that all generations would call her blessed.[17] The reasons Mary is so honored are numerous. First and foremost, as the mother of Jesus, she is Mother of God, for Jesus is fully God and fully human. As Mother of Christ, Mary is also our mother, for we are all part of Christ's body, the Church.

Catholic Tradition provides us with four Marian dogmas, or essential beliefs about Mary. In addition to our belief in Mary as Mother of God, we believe in her perpetual virginity, her Immaculate Conception, and her bodily assumption into heaven after her death.

Catholics believe that Mary was a virgin before and after the birth of Christ.[18] Mary's physical intactness was a sign of her faith, fully intact because of God's grace. Protestants sometimes attempt to use Scripture to argue against the idea of Mary's perpetual virginity, claiming that Scripture says Mary had other sons.[19] In actuality, the term used for "brothers" in this verse is an Old Testament expression for close relations. In addition, when he was on the cross, Jesus would not have needed to entrust Mary to John's care if he had other siblings who could care for her.[20]

The Immaculate Conception is a term that many misunderstand. Some Catholics mistakenly believe this term refers to the conception of Jesus, but it actually refers to the belief that Mary was conceived free from original sin. Christians have a long history of belief in the sinlessness of Mary. In fact, before the Protestant Reformation in the 1500s, no one questioned the idea that Mary was sinless. Here's why: The early Christians understood Mary as the "new Eve." While the first woman and man brought sin into the world, a special woman (Mary) and the God-man (Jesus) brought salvation. This is predicted in the Book of Genesis, when God says, "I will put enmity between you and the woman."[21] The word "woman" as it is used here is an archetypal term meaning not only Eve, but Mary as well. Secondly, Mary is known as the "Ark of the New Covenant."

In the Old Testament, the Ark of the Covenant was a specially designed box made of wood and lined with gold. It carried the Ten Commandments tablets Moses had received from God. It also carried the presence of God. For this reason, it had to be made perfectly, with no flaws. In Revelation 12, a "woman" is described, clothed with the sun and with a crown of twelve stars. She is about to give birth to one who will rule all nations. Satan is described as a dragon waiting to hurt the child after he is born. It's pretty easy to figure out that the child is Jesus, so that makes the "woman" Mary. (Because Scripture describes Mary as having a crown and being in heaven already, this is one place where we get our

Catholic understanding of Mary as Queen of Heaven, and the idea that she was assumed, body and soul, into heaven.) This passage in Revelation 12 follows a description in Revelation 11 of the Ark of the Covenant. It's obvious that the Holy Spirit wants us to make a connection here. The ark carried the presence of God under the Old Covenant, and Mary carried the presence of God (Jesus) under the New Covenant. She is the Ark of the New Covenant. But to carry the presence of God, she must be without any flaws.

Finally, in Luke 1, the angel Gabriel calls Mary "full of grace" (*Douay-Rheims Bible*). (This is where we get the beginning of the "Hail Mary" prayer.) Grace is the share of God's own life that grants us the ability to do what God asks us to do. We have received grace through our baptism and continue to receive grace through the sacraments, such as the Eucharist and reconciliation. But none of us is "full of grace." In 2 Corinthians, when Paul complains about a problem that keeps coming up for him (we don't hear exactly what the problem is), God answers, "my grace is sufficient for you." In other words, Paul has enough grace to be a good Christian, but even he does not have the fullness of grace. To have "fullness of grace" would mean always doing what God wants. That would be essential for the mother of the Son of God.

Mary didn't earn the grace granted to her by God. He made her sinless for a special purpose. She was human just as we are. In fact, Jesus was her savior just as he is ours, and he was the savior of those who came before him (such as Moses and Abraham). God gave Mary the special grace that would come through Jesus in advance. He filled her with that grace so she could be a perfect mother for him. Mary's role as mother gives her a special place in the lives of all Christians. We can always depend on her motherly care, and know that she remembers us to her Son, Jesus.

Read More about It

For more information on the Church, the saints, and Mary, please see the following citations from Scripture and the *Catechism*:

The Church

    Catechism of the Catholic Church, 781-870

The Saints

    1 Corinthians 12:12-26

    Catechism of the Catholic Church, 946-953

    Hebrews 11-12:1

Mary

    Catechism of the Catholic Church, 963-975

    Luke 1:26-56

Ideas for Teaching Children about the Church, the Saints, and Mary

A child's initial experiences of the Church are at home and in the parish. Young children (ages six and under) will have a difficult time comprehending a "universal Church" until they have more knowledge about the world in general. One step toward this understanding is learning about the historical Church, especially hearing stories of the friends of Jesus in Scripture. When children are seven and older, they can begin to experience the universal Church more fully by learning about customs for celebrating Catholic feast days in other countries (Our Lady of Guadalupe in Mexico, for example).

The universality of the Church also can be illustrated by drawing an outline of a human figure on the chalkboard or a large piece of paper. Write Jesus across the head of the figure, and invite the children to name parishes, cities, states, and countries. Write the names suggested by the children in various places all around the figure. Talk about how Christians all over the world form "one body."

You also may arrange a "pen pal" relationship between your class and a class of children the same age at another parish.

Our Church has so many images and rich traditions surrounding the saints, especially our Blessed Mother, that it's easy to introduce saints to children very early by calling them "friends of Jesus" or "heroes of God" and using pictures, holy cards, and statues. Prayers to the saints are also appropriate as children are able to understand them.

Have a party for All Saints Day. Ask the children to dress as their favorite saint, and include saint-themed games and activities.

Make a rosary using large beads, string, and a cross. (For an easier version, make a one-decade rosary.) Talk about the mysteries of the Rosary and how they help us learn about the lives of Mary and Jesus.

II.

Second Task of Catechesis

We Celebrate: Liturgical Education

Part One: Sacraments of Initiation

"Catechesis is thus a fundamental element of Christian initiation and is closely connected with the sacraments of initiation, especially with Baptism, 'the sacrament of faith.' The link uniting catechesis and Baptism is true profession of faith, which is at once an element inherent in this sacrament and the goal of catechesis."

General Directory for Catechesis, 66

For the Catechist / Questions for Reflection

- What do I remember (or what have I been told) about my baptism?

- What does my baptism mean to me today?

- What gifts of the Holy Spirit do I see present in my life?

- How does receiving Jesus in the Eucharist affect my life outside the Mass?

Sacraments — Signs and Vehicles of God's Grace

The *Catechism of the Catholic Church* defines "sacraments" as "efficacious signs of grace, instituted by Christ and entrusted to the Church, by which divine life is dispensed to us."[22] God wants to share his very life with us. He does this through his people — the Church — and the sacraments, established by Christ, that the Church celebrates. Sacramental celebrations are signs of God's grace, and they bestow God's grace as well. For the children at our parish, we define a sacrament as "a celebration we can see that reminds us God is with us." We add that the sacraments were begun by Jesus and give us grace. Grace is defined as "a share of God's own life that gives us the ability to do what God asks us to do."

There are seven sacraments: baptism, confirmation, the Eucharist, reconciliation, anointing of the sick, matrimony, and holy orders. Baptism, confirmation, and the Eucharist are called "Sacraments of Initiation" because they are the celebrations by which one enters into the life of the Church.

Baptism

In the sacrament of baptism, we enter into the "paschal mystery" of Christ. In other words, we are spiritually joined to Christ's death, burial, and resurrection. In the celebration of the sacrament, we die to sin, are buried with Christ, and raised up to live a new life in Christ.[23] The individual being baptized is immersed in water (or water is poured over his or her head) with the words, "I baptize you in the name of the Father, and of the Son, and of the Holy Spirit."

Typically, baptism is also accompanied by rites that highlight the meaning of the sacrament. The baptized is anointed with blessed oil, called "chrism." This signifies the gift of the Holy Spirit and the reality that all of us who have put on Christ in baptism share in his work as priest, prophet, and king. We are called to serve and to proclaim the Word of God, and we are adopted sons and daughters of the king, making us part of the royal family. A white garment is placed on the newly baptized, signifying the truth that he or she has put on Christ and is now free from the stain of sin. A baptismal candle is lit from the Easter candle (which represents Christ), showing that the newly baptized has received the light of Christ and is welcomed into the Church to participate with her in being the "light of the world."

Confirmation

In the sacrament of confirmation, we experience an important extension of our baptism, and the confirmation liturgy begins with a renewal of baptismal promises. The principal signs used in confirmation are the laying on of hands and the anointing with sacred chrism. From the time of the apostles, the Church has used the sign of laying on of hands to impart the gift of the Holy Spirit that completes baptism.[24]

Generally, it is the bishop, the successor of the apostles, who presides over confirmation and lays hands on those to be confirmed. He anoints them with chrism and says, "Be sealed with the gifts of the Holy Spirit." The spiritual seal to which these words refer is a permanent mark on the soul that signifies a total belonging to Christ, eternal enrollment in his service, and promise of divine protection.[25]

Confirmation increases and deepens the grace first received at baptism. It enables us to better approach God as Father, strengthens our bond with Christ, "increases the gifts of the Holy Spirit in us," binds us more closely with the Church, and "gives us a special strength of the Holy Spirit to spread and defend the faith by word and action."[26]

The gifts of the Holy Spirit that are strengthened at confirmation are wisdom, understanding, counsel, fortitude, knowledge, piety, and fear of the Lord.[27] These gifts are like seeds that, if allowed to grow in our lives, will bear the "fruits of the Spirit": charity, joy, peace, patience, kindness, goodness, generosity, gentleness, faithfulness, modesty, self-control, and chastity.[28]

Eucharist

The sacrament of the Eucharist is so vital to the Church that the Second Vatican Council called it the "fount and apex of the whole Christian life."[29] To understand why the Eucharist is so important, it is helpful to understand what Christ himself, and the Church after him, have taught about the sacrament.

Jesus taught that his flesh and blood were "food indeed."[30] Our Lord, who frequently spoke in metaphors, seemed to go out of his way with repetition to emphasize the fact that he intended the Eucharist to be understood *literally*: He was giving himself to us as food and drink. This was difficult even for his followers to understand, and some left him,[31] but

Jesus did not try to stop them by offering an alternative explanation, an indication that they understood what he meant but could not accept it.

One key to understanding Jesus' offering of himself as food is the Passover celebration of the Old Testament. The Israelites were commanded to eat the flesh of the Passover lamb that was sacrificed to save them.[32] Passover was intended to prepare God's people for Jesus, the "Lamb of God" who would be sacrificed to save us from the bondage of sin. In fact, Saint Paul calls Jesus "our paschal lamb."[33] On the night he was betrayed, Jesus ate the Passover meal with his disciples, offering the bread and the cup with the words "This is my body" and "This is my blood."[34] He asked the disciples to do what he did in his memory,[35] and the Church continues to celebrate this meal in the Mass.

We believe that Jesus becomes physically present to us under the signs of bread and wine in the Eucharistic celebration. At the moment of consecration, when the priest repeats the words of Christ at the Last Supper, the bread and wine are changed completely into Jesus' Body and Blood. Saint Paul cautions against receiving Communion without recognizing the Body and Blood of Christ,[36] highlighting the importance of this teaching.

So why does Jesus give himself to us as food? Jesus promised the Church that he would be with us always, and he is present in a most complete and literal way through the Eucharist. He wants to be intimately connected with us, and through the Eucharist, he literally becomes a part of us. It has been said that "you are what you eat," and this is especially true of our Eucharistic meal. As we partake of the body of Christ, we are formed as the body of Christ, and we are sent out to be the body of Christ in the world. Our memorial of Jesus' sacrifice is made complete by our willingness to be as Christ to others.

Ideas for Teaching Children about Sacraments of Initiation

The concept of a sacrament is a difficult one for young children (under age seven) to comprehend. Still, they can understand that sacraments are special times in the Church. Most Catholic children are baptized in infancy, so it's appropriate to talk to young children about their baptism and how it welcomed them into the Church. Education about other sacraments of initiation follows a natural progression as children prepare to celebrate them.

Go on a class visit to the baptismal font in your church. Have the children bless themselves with holy water, and talk about how this water also was used in their baptism. For children who have already reached the age of reason (about seven or older), you may wish to review (or give them an opportunity to renew) their baptismal promises.

Purchase several small gift boxes (one for each student) and small bows. On small pieces of paper, have children draw pictures (or write words) illustrating each of the gifts of the Spirit that are received at confirmation. Place these "gifts" in the box, and place the bow on top.

Act out the Communion procession in the classroom, demonstrating the correct way to receive the Eucharist. Incorporate the responses said during Mass into the class session, particularly during circle times. You may wish to begin a prayer time with "The Lord be with you," to which the children should answer, "And also with you."

Read More about It

For more information on the sacraments of initiation, please see the following citations from Scripture and the *Catechism*:

Catechism of the Catholic Church, 1210-1419

Romans 6:1-14

John 6:22-59

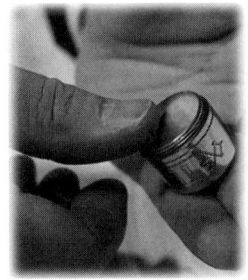

Part Two: Sacraments of Healing

"Those who are well have no need of a physician, but those who are sick; I came not to call the righteous, but sinners."

MARK 2:17

"Those who approach the sacrament of Penance obtain pardon from the mercy of God for the offense committed against Him and are at the same time reconciled with the Church, which they have wounded by their sins, and which by charity, example, and prayer seeks their conversion. By the sacred anointing of the sick and the prayer of her priests the whole Church commends the sick to the suffering and glorified Lord, asking that He may lighten their suffering and save them."

LUMEN GENTIUM, 11

For the Catechist / Questions for Reflection

- In what ways have I experienced God's healing?

- What was Jesus' attitude toward those who were ill, both with physical infirmities and illnesses of the soul?

- Is it possible for good to come from suffering?

The Great Physician

Jesus described himself as a physician who came to heal the sick. Indeed, many came to him to be cured of physical illnesses, but Jesus was most concerned with the soul. Jesus often linked the physical healings he performed with the forgiveness of sins.[37] This was because he intended physical healings to be a sign of the healing of the soul. Jesus gave his disciples the authority to forgive sins and sent them to heal the sick.[38] The Church continues Christ's ministry of healing in the sacraments of reconciliation and anointing of the sick.[39]

The Sacrament of Reconciliation

For many adults, discussion of the sacrament of reconciliation, or "confession," evokes feelings of anxiety. We may picture dark, foreboding confessionals or remember feelings of shame or guilt associated with our experiences of confession in childhood. In recent years, the Church has worked to change both the form of and instruction concerning this sacrament to make it the positive experience of unconditional love that God intends it to be. First and foremost, reconciliation should be a powerful reminder that God loves us "no matter what." It is a tangible sign of God's desire to reach out to us, even in our sinfulness, and help us reconcile ourselves with him and our brothers and sisters and repair the damage done by sin.

Sin disrupts our relationship with God and with the community. Jesus illustrated the communal aspect of forgiveness of sins when he forgave those who had alienated themselves from others, such as Zacchaeus the tax collector and Mary the prostitute, and helped them rejoin the community.[40] In the sacrament of reconciliation, the priest represents both Christ and the Christian community, a sign of the restoration of our relationship with God and our fellowship with one another.

The *Catechism of the Catholic Church* describes two major elements of the sacrament of reconciliation: our actions and God's actions.[41] Our actions consist of contrition, or feeling truly sorry for our sin; confession of our sin to the priest; and satisfaction, or doing what we can to repair the damage we have done through sin. God's actions in the sacrament include restoring us to his grace and reconciling us to himself and to the Church.

There are three forms of the sacrament of reconciliation.[42] Most often, the penitent (the person confessing) meets with the priest individually. The priest welcomes and blesses the penitent and may read from Scripture. The penitent then confesses his or her sins to the priest. The priest gives the penitent a penance (a special job to help repair the damage done by the sins confessed), then says the words of absolution. The rite ends with a prayer of thanksgiving and praise and a blessing by the priest.

When the sacrament is celebrated in a communal context, the people gather together to listen to God's Word and make an examination of conscience. The assembly may sing songs and pray the Act of Contrition together. Individual confessions are then celebrated.

In a third form of the rite, communal celebration with general confession and general absolution, sins are not confessed individually to the priest, but the priest grants absolution to the whole assembly. This form is meant to be used only in conditions of grave necessity (such as an impending disaster or other very special circumstances).

Baptism imparts to us God's free gift of forgiveness. But each of us continues to make unloving choices at times. God desires to be close to us and to help us in loving him and others. The sacrament of reconciliation is like a gift that can be opened again and again. God's mercy and forgiveness are ever present, and ever new.

Anointing of the Sick

Through the anointing of the sick, the Church community surrounds those who are gravely ill with support and brings their illnesses to God. Like reconciliation, anointing of the sick is a continuation of Jesus' healing ministry. When the sacrament is celebrated, the seriously ill are anointed on the forehead and hands with blessed oil. The priest says "Through this anointing may the Lord in his love and mercy help you with the grace of the Holy Spirit. May the Lord who frees you from sin save you and raise you up."[43]

Anointing of the sick may be received by anyone who is seriously ill. It is not necessary that the individual be at the point of death. The sacrament can be celebrated multiple times, even for the same illness.

The effects of anointing of the sick are described by the *Catechism:* 1) The seriously ill person is granted grace and strengthening as a gift of the Holy Spirit. This is meant to facilitate healing of the soul, and of the body if it is God's will. 2) The suffering of the person is united with Christ's suffering, enabling the person who is ill to participate in the saving work of Christ. 3) By uniting their suffering with that of Christ, those who celebrate this sacrament contribute to the good of the Church, and the Church (including the communion of saints) in turn prays for them. 4) The seriously ill person is prepared for the final journey through death into new life. "The Anointing of the Sick completes our conformity to the death and Resurrection of Christ, just as Baptism began it."[44]

Anointing of the sick is ideally celebrated within the context of the Eucharist with the entire Christian community.[45] This offers the most complete sign of the personal and communal dimensions of the sacrament. It also brings the Christian community closer together, for we draw closer to one another and to God as we "bear one another's burdens, and so fulfill the law of Christ."[46]

Read More about It

For more information on the sacraments of healing, please see the following citations from Scripture and the *Catechism*:

Catechism of the Catholic Church, 1420-1532

1 John 1:8

John 20:23

James 5:14-15

Ideas for Teaching Children about the Sacraments of Healing

As previously mentioned, children have difficulty with the concept of sin until their thinking becomes more rule-based (around age seven). That's why we typically prepare children for the sacrament of reconciliation around that age (or shortly thereafter). The more general discussions of sacraments inherent in preparation for First Communion and First Reconciliation offer an ideal time to discuss anointing of the sick as well.

Visit the place in your church where reconciliation is celebrated. Explain to the children where the priest and penitent sit, and talk about how the sacramental celebration unfolds. This takes some of the mystery out of what happens in the reconciliation room and helps children learn the form of the sacrament.

Take the children to the church and show them the aumbry (the place where the holy oils are stored). Talk about the significance of each type of oil, with special attention to the oil used for the anointing of the sick.

Part Three: Sacraments at the Service of Communion

"It is also important that every means should be used to encourage vocations to the Priesthood, and to the different forms of consecration to God in religious and apostolic life."

GENERAL DIRECTORY FOR CATECHESIS, 86

"Those of the faithful who are consecrated by Holy Orders are appointed to feed the Church in Christ's name with the word and the grace of God. Finally, Christian spouses, in virtue of the sacrament of Matrimony, whereby they signify and partake of the mystery of that unity and fruitful love which exists between Christ and His Church, help each other to attain to holiness in their married life and in the rearing and education of their children. By reason of their state and rank in life they have their own special gift among the people of God."

LUMEN GENTIUM, 11

For the Catechist / Questions for Reflection

- What qualities make a good priest?

- How is marriage a sign of the love between Christ and the Church?

The Sacrament of Holy Orders

The *Catechism* defines holy orders as "the sacrament through which the mission entrusted by Christ to his apostles continues to be exercised in the Church until the end of time."[47] Through the celebration of the sacrament, men who have been called by God to serve the Church consecrate their lives to this task.

Throughout Scripture, we find references to those who are consecrated to God's service. Priests of the Old Covenant approached God on behalf of the people and offered sacrifices for the forgiveness of their sins.[48] Priests also made offerings of thanksgiving to God.[49] Early in Scripture we read of Melchizedek, who offers bread and wine in thanksgiving to God. The Letter to the Hebrews in the New Testament refers to Melchizedek as prefiguring (or foreshadowing) the priesthood of Christ.[50] When the time came for him to return to the Father, Christ entrusted his mission to the apostles.

There are three degrees of the sacrament of holy orders: episcopal ordination (ordination of bishops), the ordination of priests, and the ordination of deacons.

The bishop, as an immediate successor of the apostles, represents Christ as teacher, shepherd, and priest.[51] Just as Christ came to be the servant of all, the bishop is the chief servant of the people of his diocese, and as shepherd is charged with their care. Priests are the bishops' co-workers in the apostolic mission of Christ.[52] Priests depend on their bishop and must work in communion with him. Deacons are ordained for service. Presiding over the Eucharistic liturgy is reserved for the priesthood, but deacons often assist during the celebration of the Eucharist. They also bless marriages, proclaim the Gospel, preach homilies, preside over funerals, baptize infants, and perform works of charity.[53]

The celebration of the sacrament of holy orders includes the bishop's laying of hands on those to be ordained. The bishop says a prayer of consecration asking for God to pour out his Holy Spirit in a special way and confer the gifts the candidate will need to do the work to which he is called. Those ordained as bishops or priests are anointed with chrism to symbolize the anointing of the Holy Spirit. The ring, the miter (special hat), and the crosier (shepherd's staff) are given to the bishop as signs of his mission to proclaim the Word of God, his faithfulness to the Church, and his role as shepherd of the faithful. Priests are presented with the paten and chalice (used in the Liturgy of the Eucharist). Deacons are presented with the Book of the Gospels to symbolize their mission to proclaim Christ.[54]

While we all share in the priesthood of Christ by virtue of our baptism, the ministerial priesthood is unique in that bishops and priests are at the service of all the faithful.[55] The priest represents Christ, who made himself the servant of all. Just as the one redemptive sacrifice "accomplished once for all" is made present in the Eucharistic sacrifice of the Church, "the same is true of the one priesthood of Christ; it is made present through the ministerial priesthood without diminishing the uniqueness of Christ's priesthood."[56] Because the priest represents Christ, he also represents the whole Church, the Body of Christ, when presenting the prayer of the Church,[57] just as the priests of the Old Covenant represented God's people as a whole. The priesthood is a special gift of God to his people — a visible sign of Christ's presence, his leadership, and his service.

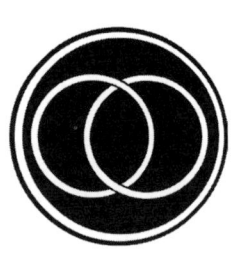

The Sacrament of Matrimony

The history of the sacrament of matrimony begins with the story of the creation of the first man and woman, found in the Book of Genesis. In reading this account, we come to understand that man and woman were created for one another, in the image of God himself. After God gives them to one another, they are "no longer two, but one flesh."[58] They are commanded by God to "be fruitful and multiply," and the expression of love between them becomes something tangible — a person.

In this first story of marriage we find some important principles that have characterized the Church's teachings on the sacrament of matrimony. One important principle is that men and women are created in the image of God. The *Catechism* states that any discord or disorder in marriage is not a consequence of human nature, but of sin.[59] Another point made by the *Catechism* is that in the sacrament of matrimony, a man and woman are mysteriously joined as one. This unity is permanent; they are "no longer two." Finally, a sacramental marriage is a fruitful one. Because men and women are made for one another in the image of God, their mutual love becomes an image of the intimacy between the persons of the Trinity — a love that creates and bears fruit. This creative love is seen most concretely in the birth of children, but the *Catechism* points out that even couples who have not been blessed with children can bear fruit through their charity, hospitality, and sacrifice.[60]

In the celebration of the sacrament of matrimony, a man and a woman express their consent before the Church to enter into a new "oneness" forever. It is the expression of consent given through the marriage vows that is the essential element of the sacrament.[61] The priest or deacon then receives the consent of the spouses in the name of the Church. Though the celebration of the sacrament, the marriage bond is sealed by God, and the couple is granted the grace to form one another in holiness and to welcome and educate their children.[62]

As God's covenant with his people unfolded over time, so did the understanding of godly marriage. We see this in Jesus' Sermon on the Mount as he calls married persons to greater holiness, a holiness that would ultimately be made possible through the grace that would flow from his death and resurrection. Under the New Covenant, marriage also becomes an image of Christ's love for his Church. Chapter Five of Saint Paul's letter to the Ephesians describes a relationship of mutual self-sacrifice. Wives are asked to submit to their husbands, and husbands are asked to love their wives as Christ loved the Church — with his whole self. Just as Christ does not withhold any good thing from his Church, but is its chief servant, so must be the attitude of husbands toward their wives. For both husbands and wives, self-will must die in the service of unity. This is the foundation of Christian marriage — and indeed the Christian life. We are called to die to ourselves in order to find a greater joy than we have ever known. "For whoever would save his life will lose it, and whoever loses his life for my sake will find it."[63]

Read More about It

For more information on the sacraments of vocation, please see the following citations from Scripture and the *Catechism*:

Catechism of the Catholic Church, 1533-1666

Hebrews 4:14-6:20

Genesis 1:26-31

Ephesians 5:21-33

Ideas for Teaching Children about the Sacraments at the Service of Communion

An ideal time to discuss the sacraments of vocation in depth is the teen years, when kids are grappling with their own sense of identity and asking important questions such as "Who am I?" and "Why am I here?"

Younger children also can be introduced to these sacraments. Contact your diocesan office of vocations to obtain names and addresses of seminarians in your diocese. Have your class "adopt a seminarian" by choosing someone to pray for and write to. The children may enjoy making Christmas and/or Easter cards for your "adopted seminarian."

Ask your priest to visit your class when you talk about the sacrament of holy orders. Have the children prepare some questions in advance, asking him when he first felt called to the priesthood and what he likes about being a priest.

Ask the children to bring a wedding photograph of their parents to the class session in which you discuss the sacrament of matrimony. Talk about the promises husbands and wives make to one another in the celebration of the sacrament and the grace God gives married couples to help them live together as a family.

III.

Third Task of Catechesis

We Love: Moral Formation

"Conversion to Jesus Christ implies walking in his footsteps. Catechesis must, therefore, transmit to the disciples the attitudes of the Master himself.... Evangelization, which 'involves the proclamation and presentation of morality,' displays all the force of its appeal where it offers not only the proclaimed word but the lived word too. This moral testimony, which is prepared for by catechesis, must always demonstrate the social consequences of the demands of the Gospel."

General Directory for Catechesis, 85

For the Catechist / Questions for Reflection

- What does it mean to be a moral person?

- How do our "actions speak louder than words" when it comes to moral principles?

- Who in my life has been a strong example of a moral person?

God has created humanity in his image and likeness. We have been given the gift of reason, whereby we understand the order of things established by God,[64] and recognize the voice of God, urging us to do good and avoid evil. When we live moral lives, we testify to the dignity we have been given by virtue of the fact that we are created in God's image.[65]

God affirms our dignity by giving us free will, but freedom can only truly be realized when it is used to do what is good and right.[66] Through Christ, we are delivered from sin and temptation and freed to live the lives for which we were created.[67] With this freedom, then, comes responsibility.[68]

Both the charity to which we are called and the inheritance we are offered are outlined by Christ in the Beatitudes. Under the old covenant, God promised to bless Abraham and his descendants and to make their name great.[69] Under the new covenant, Christ echoes these promises by announcing the blessing of those who live lives of charity and humility.[70] To them he promises the kingdom of heaven, inheritance of the earth, and the title "sons of God."[71]

According to the *Catechism*, whether or not an act is moral is dependent on the object chosen, the intention, and the circumstances of the action.[72] For an action to be morally good, it must involve a good object, good intentions, and the proper circumstances. Good intentions alone do not make an action just. "The end does not justify the means."[73] When determining the rightness of an action, we should be led by a conscience[74] that has been informed by God's rules of moral living and is guided by the Holy Spirit. We should always obey the certain judgment of our own conscience,[75] but we have the responsibility to make sure our conscience has been well formed. We form our conscience through lifelong study of God's Word and the teachings of the Church, aided by the guidance of the Holy Spirit and the advice of brothers and sisters in Christ.[76]

A focus on good things,[77] together with education, action, perseverance, and cooperation with divine grace,[78] helps us to grow in virtue, which is defined by the *Catechism* as "an habitual and firm disposition to do the good."[79] Scripture and the *Catechism* point to four virtues on which all others depend: prudence, justice, fortitude, and temperance.[80] Prudence is the ability to discern the good in every circumstance,[81] to know how to do "the right thing at the right time." Justice is the will to give what is due to God and to each person.[82] Fortitude helps us to resist temptation and to persevere in the face of hardship and struggle.[83]

"Commandments Fulfilled in the Gospel"

Jesus' teachings on living a moral life might be summarized in two important points. One is that *morality comes from the heart*. He chastised the Pharisees and other teachers for retaining (and extrapolating upon) the letter of God's law while at the same time losing the spirit of the law. For example, at the time of Christ, many rules had been developed concerning proper observance of the sabbath. So many, in fact, that one seemingly had to work very hard to keep the sabbath as a day of rest! Jesus spoke out against burdens such as these that had been placed upon people in the name of following God's laws, and instead challenged people to attend to the content of their hearts. In doing so, Jesus was not abolishing the Old Law; rather he was fulfilling it by taking it to a higher level.[84] For example, he reminded his listeners of the commandment against adultery, then said, "I say to you that every one who looks at a woman lustfully has already committed adultery with her in his heart.[85] Jesus called his listeners to something beyond a change in behavior; he called them to a conversion of the heart.

Another key point of Jesus' moral teaching is that *morality is rooted in love*. The Law of Moses was a preparation for the Gospel. The New Law given by Christ perfects the Old. It is a Law of Love.[86] When asked about the greatest commandment, Jesus replied "You shall love the Lord your God with all your heart, and with all your soul, and with all your mind. This is the great and first commandment. And a second is like it: You shall love your neighbor as yourself. On these two commandments depend all the law and the prophets."[87]

The Ten Commandments

The Ten Commandments[88] serve as a basic guideline for the rules of godly living. To more accurately grasp the meaning of the Ten Commandments, it is useful to look at them within the context of love of God and love of others. As Jesus said, all of the commandments relate to these two principles.

The first three commandments relate to loving God. "You shall have no other gods before me" refers not only to worship of other gods, but is an admonition to put God above all other things in our lives. The second commandment, "You shall not take the name of the Lord your God in vain," reminds us to keep God's name holy. This commandment is not just about using God's name as profanity. It reminds us to treat God's name with honor and respect and avoid bringing disrepute to God's name by taking false oaths or uttering blasphemy. The third commandment, to keep the sabbath day holy, is truly a gift from God. Under the Old Covenant, the Jewish people observed Saturday as a day to rest and give

thanks to God for his goodness. The *Catechism* states: "The sabbath, which represented the completion of the first creation, has been replaced by Sunday which recalls the new creation inaugurated by the Resurrection of Christ."[89] We can easily get caught up in the hectic pace of life and forget what life is all about. For this reason, we are commanded by God to take a break and appreciate him and his creation. In canon law and the *Catechism*, Sunday is called the "foremost holy day of obligation." We gather together on Sunday to give thanks to God in the Eucharist and to remember who we are as a people.

The fourth through tenth commandments relate to loving others. The fourth commandment calls us to honor our parents, but also informs our relationships with others. We are called to honor each person as an individual with inherent dignity, created in God's image. Concerning the fifth commandment, Jesus said, "You have heard that it was said to the men of old, 'You shall not kill; and whoever kills shall be liable to judgment.' But I say to you that every one who is angry with his brother shall be liable to judgment."[90] Again challenging us to go past behavior itself to the attitudes of the heart, Jesus points out that we cannot be the people God created us to be when we create barriers between ourselves and others by feeding our anger or refusing to forgive. The commandments themselves call us to an examination of the heart when we are told not only to avoid adultery (sixth commandment), but also to avoid lust (tenth commandment). The root of sinful sexual behavior is the objectification of the body, looking at ourselves or others as "things" to be used, rather than beings created by God. The seventh and ninth commandments call us to avoid theft (seventh commandment), but again go further to address the attitude that would give rise to theft (ninth commandment). We should be happy with what we have, knowing that God has blessed each of us in many ways. Finally, the eighth commandment, "You shall not bear false witness against your neighbor,"[91] calls us to live in and bear witness to the truth and to build one another up, rather than injuring the reputation of others.

Virtue and the Work of the Holy Spirit

We grow in our ability to live a moral life as we accept the truth about ourselves as beings created in God's image. We are created to be like God, which is the goal of a virtuous life.[92] Through the Holy Spirit's work within us and the grace God gives us in the sacraments, we grow in our love for God and others and, consequently, in virtuous behavior. It is a formation of the heart, rooted in love, directed by God.

Read More about It

For more information on Catholic morality, please see the following citations from Scripture and the *Catechism*:

> *Catechism of the Catholic Church*, 1691-2557

> *Exodus* 20

> *Matthew* 5-7

Ideas for Teaching Children about Morality

We introduce basic principles of Christian morality to young children when we talk about being kind to one another or about helping their moms and dads at home, and when we give children guidelines about how to treat one another in class. As children reach the age of reason, they are better able to understand the concept of right and wrong and learn about moral decision-making.

Use hypothetical situations children face at home or school to discuss moral decision-making. Here are some examples:

• You are in the middle of watching a TV show, and your mother tells you to clean your room.

• You are playing soccer with your friends at recess when you notice a new kid who has no one to play with.

Ask the children to act out the situations and show what choice God would want them to make.

You also may play a game in which children are asked to match hypothetical situations (such as the ones above) to the Ten Commandments.

IV.

Fourth Task of Catechesis

We Pray: Conversation with God

"When catechesis is permeated by a climate of prayer, the assimilation of the entire Christian life reaches its summit."

GENERAL DIRECTORY FOR CATECHESIS, 85

For the Catechist / Questions for Reflection

- What are some different ways to pray? Which do I use most often?

_____

_____

_____

- When am I most likely to pray?

_____

_____

_____

- In which environments does prayer come most naturally to me?

_____

_____

What is Prayer?

Quoting Saint John Damascene, the *Catechism of the Catholic Church* defines prayer as "the raising of one's mind and heart to God or the requesting of good things from God."[93] Prayer is being in the presence of God and in communion with him.[94] It is the mystery within which we believe, celebrate, and live our faith.[95] Prayer is our response to the call of a loving God. He calls us through nature, other people, and our very hearts and minds. As he calls us, we answer his call through prayer.

Jesus Christ is the "one mediator" between God and humanity.[96] As Christians, we approach God the Father through Christ by virtue of a covenant relationship between God and his people that has unfolded throughout history. Prayer is the expression of that covenant relationship.

Sacred Scripture and Sacred Tradition provide us with a rich variety of models of prayer. The conversations between God and Abraham, the beautiful poetry of the Psalms, the perfect prayer of Jesus, the words and witness of the saints; all are part of a treasure trove of prayer we have inherited.

Still, certain qualities are common to all Christian prayer. In Christ, we are all joined as one body of believers. Therefore, all prayer is simultaneously both individual and communal. Our personal prayers are joined to those of the whole Church, including the saints who have gone before us. Our traditional "family prayers," such as the ones we use in Mass, are outward expressions of our unity in prayer. Another quality common to all Christian prayer is that it is by nature conversational. In the book *The Way of Prayer*, Pope John Paul II states: "When we hold a conversation with someone, we not only speak, but we also listen. Prayer, therefore, is also listening." Prayerful listening can include quiet time in meditation or reflection. It also can include attentiveness to God's creation, teachers in the faith, or Holy Scripture.

Responding to God's call through prayer can take many forms. Saint Augustine once said, "He who sings prays twice." Saint Thérèse of Lisieux taught us that even the littlest, everyday things we do can be offered as prayer to God. In this way, we can make our daily lives a constant prayer of praise and thanksgiving.

Spontaneous prayer helps us to develop the unique relationship God desires with each of us. A consideration of the forms of prayer discussed in the *Catechism of the Catholic Church* can help us to formulate our own spontaneous prayers:[97]

Blessing is our acceptance of the gifts of God. We recognize God as the source of all good things, and we bless him for blessing us. **Adoration** is the form of prayer in which we recognize our state before God. We express our understanding of him as Creator and ourselves as created beings. Adoration is realizing that, but for his amazing love for each of us, we would be nothing before him.

Without God, we have nothing. Prayers of **petition** or supplication express understanding of this relationship by asking God for the things we need. Scripture teaches that the Holy Spirit himself intercedes for us when we do not know what to pray.[98] Prayers of petition begin with acknowledging our sinfulness and asking God for his forgiveness. The *Catechism* states that asking for forgiveness is the "prerequisite for both the Eucharistic liturgy and personal prayer." Approaching God in humility reestablishes our communion with him and with one another and makes us better able to ask according to his will. This is important, because at the center of Christian petition is the "desire and search for the kingdom to come."[99] No one knows what is best for us better than God, who made us. God is able to see our present and our future and how choices and events fit into the "big picture." Therefore, it is only fitting for us to pray, "not my will, but yours be done."

God is delighted when we approach him as his children and ask for the things we need. We should feel free to ask him for anything at any time. Jesus describes him as a loving Father who cares deeply for us and pays attention to even the smallest of our needs. "What man of you, if his son asks him for bread, will give him a stone?" he asks. "How much more will your Father who is in heaven give good things to those who ask him!"[100]

Intercession is prayer on behalf of someone else. A common example of intercession is praying for someone who is sick. Attending to the needs of others is a vital part of the Christian life. Intercession should be a part of both personal and communal prayer. Scripture encourages us to pray often for others, including our leaders and even our enemies.[101]

Prayers of **thanksgiving** extol God for what he has done. Like supplication, thanksgiving recognizes that God is the source of all good gifts. Prayers of thanksgiving also help us recognize the blessings in our lives and focus on what we have, rather than what we are lacking.

Praise is the form of prayer that recognizes God simply for who he is, rather than what he has done.[102] In prayers of praise we give God glory. The *Catechism* states: "Praise embraces the other forms of prayer and carries them toward him who is its source and goal."

We often use multiple forms in the same prayer, and find examples of this in Scripture (the Our Father, for example). But no matter what form we use, we should remember that God is always listening, calling us ever closer to him.

Read More about It

For more information on prayer, please see the following citations from Scripture and the *Catechism*:

Catechism of the Catholic Church, 2558-2865

Matthew 6:5-15

Ideas for Teaching Children about Prayer

Children are never too young to learn to pray. Very young children (toddlers and two-year-olds) will benefit a great deal from the use of pictures and statues. They may be encouraged to say "Hi" or "I love you" to Jesus depicted in a statue or painting. They can be taught to make the Sign of the Cross (an especially good prayer for your children, because of its movement and brevity) and to sing songs to God.

Older children should be taught both our traditional Catholic prayers and the art of spontaneous prayer. Traditional prayers are valuable because they enable us to pray together, in unison, as God's people. They highlight our unity of faith and purpose. Traditional prayers also give us a repertoire from which to choose when we are not sure what to pray. Traditional prayers should be introduced gradually as children are able to understand them. We should not ask children to pray what they cannot understand, because without understanding they can't mean what they are praying.

Make some time for prayer during each group session. Set a theme for the prayer each week by choosing one of the forms of prayer to use. Create a prayerful environment by sitting in a circle and lighting a candle. Ask each child to say something to God using the prayer form selected (for example, "Tonight we are going to go around the circle praying for people who need God's help," or "Tonight we will thank God for something"). Use a group response to each child's prayer in the style of the Prayers of the Faithful from Mass (perhaps "Lord, hear our prayer," or, for prayers of thanksgiving, "Thank you, Lord"). Be sure to allow children to "pass" if they are uncomfortable speaking in the group, but encourage everyone to participate.

Use the liturgical calendar to generate ideas for traditional prayers to use in the classroom throughout the year. For example, use the Prayer of Saint Francis the week of his feast day, October 4. Be sure to run through a short explanation of any prayers that may be difficult for children to understand.

V. Fifth Task of Catechesis

We Are One in Christ: Education for Community Life

"Christian community life is not realized spontaneously. It is necessary to educate it carefully. In this apprenticeship, the teaching of Christ on community life, recounted in the Gospel of St. Matthew, calls for attitudes which it is for catechesis to inculcate."

GENERAL DIRECTORY FOR CATECHESIS, 86

For the Catechist / Questions for Reflection

- What are the characteristics of a community?

- What does it mean to be a responsible member of a community?

- What prepares individuals to live in a community?

Necessities of Community Life

We are called to live a life not only in communion with God, but also with one another. The early Church placed a high priority on functioning as a community, and Scripture describes believers as being "together" and having "all things in common."[103] The cohesiveness of their community helped the early Christians to face extreme persecution and fulfill Christ's mandate to "Go into all the world and preach the gospel to the whole creation."[104]

Because humans are social by nature, the good of each individual, according to the *Catechism*, is related to the common good.[105] The Second Vatican Council defined "common good" as "the sum of those conditions of social life which allow social groups and their individual members relatively thorough and ready access to their own fulfillment."[106] The common good presupposes "respect for the person," requires the "social well-being and development of the group itself," and requires peace, or "the stability and security of a just order."[107]

The *General Directory for Catechesis* draws on the teachings of Christ to list several attitudes necessary for living in community.[108] The first is "the spirit of simplicity and humility." To form a close community, we must approach others without conceit or arrogance. We must recognize that God gives everyone special gifts, and not consider ourselves better than anyone else. We must become willing to serve one another in love.

A second essential in community life is special concern for the least among us. Lewis Thomas said, "A society can be judged by the way it treats its most disadvantaged, its least beloved." Jesus said, "As you did it to one of the least of these my brethren, you did it to me."[109] We must recognize and appreciate the dignity present in each member of society and see each person as a unique being, created in God's image.

We must work to meet the needs of all, especially basic needs such as food, shelter, safety, education, and health care. A similar requirement of community life is a concern for the marginalized, those who have been alienated or who have gone astray. When we see ourselves as the "one body" described in Scripture,[110] we will not feel whole when one of our members is separated from us.

When we truly care for one another, we do not cover up wounds that need to be healed or turn our backs when someone is engaging in destructive behavior. Being loving sometimes requires us to be "painfully honest," to warn others of the harm they are doing to themselves or others and help them do better.

Common prayer is another quality of Christian community life. In communal prayer, we approach God with one voice, making our needs known to one another and to the Creator who gives us every good thing. Praying together helps us to better discern God's will for our lives and opens the community to the work of the Holy Spirit.

In any group of human beings, people are bound to have hurt feelings or misunderstandings. An attitude of mutual forgiveness and reconciliation is essential for living in communion with one another; so essential, in fact, that Jesus stated: "If you are offering your gift at the altar, and there remember that your brother has something against you, leave your gift there before the altar and go; first be reconciled to your brother, and then come and offer your gift."[111] We should approach God after we have made efforts to be reconciled with one another, for God forgives us as we forgive others.[112]

All of these important features of community life can be summed up, according to the *General Directory*, in an attitude of love for one another. When we love one another as God has loved us, we can withstand almost any obstacle, "for love covers a multitude of sins."[113]

Community and Ecumenism

Our awareness of the qualities of Christian community should lead us to pursue unity with those in other Christian traditions. This pursuit of unity begins with a clear knowledge of the faith we profess, but also an understanding for the beliefs of others. In our pursuit of unity, we must not compromise what we believe to be truth in an effort to "get along with one another," for such compromise is not true unity of faith. However, we should work to discover and celebrate the beliefs we share in common, praying for the day that God will lead us to an even deeper communion with himself and one another.

Read More about It

For more information on community, please see the following citations from Scripture and the *Catechism:*

Catechism of the Catholic Church, 1897-1948, 2179

Matthew 25:31-46

John 13:1-15

Ideas for Teaching Children about Community

Children learn about living in communities from the very beginning of their lives. The first community they experience is the family. Later, they experience community through their schools, neighborhoods, and parishes. Explicit instruction on community, by talking about and demonstrating how we should treat one another and working to identify and meet each group member's needs, should be a priority for catechists working with any age level. As children grow, their community of peers becomes more and more important in their lives. Even more emphasis should be placed on the community experience of faith in the pre-teen and teen years.

Even if your sessions are only an hour long, allow a few minutes of community-oriented "gathering time" at the beginning of each group session. Provide children with activities they can do together, such as religious-themed puzzles or games (available at many Christian bookstores).

During group times, engage the children in conversation about what is happening in their lives. Ask if they (or someone in their family) needs prayers, and include these intentions in class prayer times.

Invite ministry leaders in your parish to come to the classroom and talk with the children about how their work contributes to the parish community.

VI.
Sixth Task of Catechesis

We Are Sent: Missionary Initiation

"...catechesis promotes a lively missionary sense among believers. This is shown by clear witness to the faith, by an attitude of respect and mutual understanding, by dialogue and cooperation in defense of the rights of the person and of the poor and, where possible, with explicit proclamation of the Gospel."

GENERAL DIRECTORY FOR CATECHESIS, 200

"And he said to them, 'Go into all the world and preach the gospel to the whole creation.' "

MARK 16:15

For the Catechist / Questions for Reflection

- What are some different ways to tell others about God?

- Who in my life has been the most powerful witness of

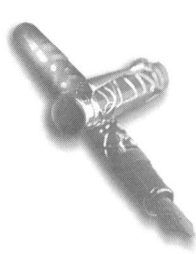

Christ's love? Why?

_____

_____

The Missionary Mandate

At the conclusion of Mass, we are told to "Go in peace to love and serve the Lord." This is a simple, yet profound, directive that signifies a great truth about what we have experienced in worship and who we are in the world. We have been fed with the Word of God in the Liturgy of the Word, and with Christ himself in the Eucharist. Consequently, we are sent to be God's Word to a world in desperate need of truth. We go out to be the Body of Christ to those who are longing for his compassion and healing. We respond "Thanks be to God," indicating our acceptance of this mission.

The *Catechism of the Catholic Church* calls mission work a requirement of the Church's catholicity,[114] meaning that because the Church is for all humanity, we must be a welcoming people, taking Christ's message to others. In fact, the Second Vatican Council called the Church "the universal sacrament of salvation."[115] We are the visible sign to the world that Christ welcomes all to life in him.

Taking Christ to the world is not only a collective responsibility, but also an individual one. In his encyclical letter *Redemptoris Missio*, Pope John Paul II calls missionary activity "a matter for all Christians." Does this mean we are called to move to a foreign land and work full time as missionaries? Perhaps, but not necessarily. Because Christ's message is for everyone, we may already be in the place where we are called to minister. Our families, friends, and co-workers all need opportunities to experience God's love and truth.

Missionary activity is directed, first and foremost, toward

those who do not know Christ or have never heard the basic Gospel message. As Catholics, we believe in a just God who would provide a way of salvation for someone who had no opportunity to hear the Gospel. This does not, however, lessen our obligation to spread the Gospel message. God's will is that all should come to know him through his Church. Because, in God's design, the Church is the primary vehicle for spreading the Good News of Christ, we are to act as if we are the only way others may come to know him. "Therefore though God in ways known to Himself can lead those inculpably ignorant of the Gospel to find that faith without which it is impossible to please Him (Hebrews 11:6), yet a necessity lies upon the Church (1 Corinthians 9:16), and at the same time a sacred duty, to preach the Gospel. And hence missionary activity today as always retains its power and necessity."[116]

Forms of the Message

There is one Gospel, but many forms of the message. The example we show others is just as important as what we say about Christ, if not more so. Highlighting this point, Saint Francis of Assisi said, "Preach the Gospel at all times … when necessary, use words." We are called to tell others about Christ through the choices we make in our daily lives — the way we treat others, the priorities we set, and the way we do our work. "For all Christians, wherever they live, are bound to show forth, by the example of their lives and by the witness of the word, that new man put on at baptism and that power of the Holy Spirit by which they have been strengthened at Confirmation."[117]

The environment in which we minister does not change the Gospel itself, but it may change the form of the message. The *General Directory for Catechesis* points out the necessity of presenting the Gospel message in its purity, but also says that it will lose much of its effectiveness if the people to whom it is being presented are not considered.[118] While we must hand on the authentic and complete message of Christ, we must be sensitive to individual and cultural needs.

In some cases, individuals or a society as a whole is not ready to hear the Gospel message directly. In these cases, according to the Second Vatican Council, we "can and must at least bear witness to Christ by charity and by works of mercy, with all patience, prudence and great confidence. Thus [we] will prepare the way for the Lord and make Him somehow present."[119]

Empowered for the Mission

We are energized for our mission in the world by God's love for us.[120] When we truly come to know God's love for us, we will naturally want to share that love with others.

The Holy Spirit, in particular, has a special role in historical and present-day mission work.[121] It was by the power of the Holy Spirit that Christ was conceived. The Spirit moved Christ to begin his ministry, and Christ sent the Spirit to the apostles at Pentecost, the birthday of the Church. The Holy Spirit continues to empower Christians today through the gifts conferred at confirmation.

Our unity as believers should also be a source of strength and witness to the faith we profess. Unfortunately, many divisions exist in the Church today, even among those who call themselves "Catholic," but especially within the Christian community as a whole. While ecumenical dialogue is a distinctly different task from spreading the Gospel to those who have not yet heard it, the nature of our mission as a Church calls us to work toward unity.[122]

The Goal of Mission Work
It is up to each of us to plant the seeds of God's Word in our world today and to point others to Christ. Jesus calls his followers "the light of the world" and "the salt of the earth."[123] Similarly, the Second Vatican Council states that it is up to the laity "to be a leaven working on the temporal order from within, to dispose it always in accordance with Christ."[124] We are called to change the world from within by identifying the goodness and truth already present in humanity and relating these positive qualities to the God who is their source.[125] We are also charged with standing against injustice and untruth in our world.

We can never know when or where the seed of God's Word may take root and grow, but this growth is God's work, not ours. We bear witness to God's love and justice in hope that others will respond, but in the end, it is the witness of Christ in the world that counts — celebrating God's love for us and giving others a chance to know him.

Read More about It
For more information on missionary work, please see the following Church documents and citations from Scripture and the *Catechism*:

Decree Ad Gentes on the Missionary Activity of the Church

Catechism of the Catholic Church, 849-856

Romans 1:16

1 Corinthians 1:17

1 Corinthians 9:16-18

You may also write the Pontifical Mission Societies, National Office, 366 Fifth Avenue, New York, N.Y. 10001.

Ideas for Teaching Children about Missionary Work

Children can be taught from an early age about how to be good examples for others, through subtle communications such as, "Who can show us how we should be listening to the Bible story?" As children grow older and begin to look more closely at their own identity and purpose, the catechist is presented with natural opportunities to teach about mission work and evangelization.

Have children discuss various ways they can teach others about God (being a good example at school, or inviting friends to parish events).

Ask the children to pray for and/or write to specific missionaries. Post a map of the world in the space where the group meets, with the location of the missionaries marked on the map.

Endnotes

1. *Catechism of the Catholic Church* (CCC), 44
2. *Gaudium et Spes*, 36
3. Acts 1:15-26
4. *Dei Verbum*, 10
5. Genesis 3:15
6. Exodus 12
7. James 2:14-17
8. CCC, 169
9. CCC, 1010-1023
10. CCC, 1861
11. 1 Corinthians 3:13-15
12. 1 Corinthians 12:27
13. CCC, 946
14. *Lumen Gentium*, 49
15. CCC, 956
16. James 5:16
17. Luke 1:48
18. CCC, 499
19. Matthew 13:55
20. John 19:25-27
21. Genesis 3:15
22. CCC, 1131
23. Romans 6:3-4
24. Acts 8:15-17
25. CCC, 1296
26. CCC, 1303
27. Isaiah 11:2
28. CCC, 1832; Galatians 5:22-23
29. *Lumen Gentium*, 11
30. John 6:55
31. John 6:60-65
32. Exodus 12:8
33. 1 Corinthians 5:7
34. Matthew 26:26-28
35. Luke 22:19
36. 1 Corinthians 11:27
37. John 20:23
38. Mark 6:12-13
39. CCC, 1421
40. CCC, 1443
41. CCC, 1448
42. CCC, 1480-1483
43. *Sacram unctionem infirmorum*
44. CCC, 1520-1523
45. CCC, 1517
46. Galatians 6:2
47. CCC, 1536
48. CCC, 1539; Hebrews 5:1; Exodus 29:1-30; Leviticus 8
49. Genesis 14:18-20
50. Hebrews 5:10, 6:20
51. CCC, 1558
52. CCC, 1562
53. CCC, 1570
54. CCC, 1574
55. CCC, 1547
56. CCC, 1545
57. CCC, 1552
58. Genesis 2:18-25
59. CCC, 1606-1608
60. CCC, 1654
61. CCC, 1626
62. CCC, 1630-1642
63. Matthew 16:25
64. CCC, 1704
65. CCC, 1706
66. CCC, 1733
67. CCC, 1708
68. CCC, 1731
69. Genesis 12:3
70. CCC, 1716-1717
71. Matthew 5:3-12
72. CCC, 1751
73. CCC, 1759
74. CCC, 1780-1785
75. CCC, 1790
76. CCC, 1785
77. Philippians 4:8; CCC, 1803
78. CCC, 1810
79. CCC, 1803
80. CCC, 1805; Wisdom 8:7

[81] CCC, 1806
[82] CCC, 1807
[83] CCC, 1808
[84] CCC, 1967-1968
[85] Matthew 5:28
[86] CCC, 1964-1972
[87] Matthew 22:37-40
[88] Exodus 20:1-17
[89] CCC, 2190
[90] Matthew 5:21-22
[91] Exodus 20:16
[92] CCC, 1803
[93] CCC, 2559
[94] CCC, 2565
[95] CCC, 2558
[96] 1 Timothy 2:5
[97] CCC, 2625-2643
[98] Romans 8:26
[99] CCC, 2631-2632
[100] Matthew 7:9-11
[101] 1 Timothy 2:1-2; Romans 12:14; CCC, 2636
[102] CCC, 2639
[103] Acts 2:44
[104] Mark 16:15
[105] CCC, 1905
[106] *Gaudium et spes*, 26
[107] CCC 1907-1909
[108] *General Directory for Catechesis*, 86
[109] Matthew 25:40
[110] 1 Corinthians 12:27
[111] Matthew 5:23-24
[112] Matthew 6:14
[113] 1 Peter 4:8
[114] CCC, 849-856
[115] *Lumen Gentium*, 48
[116] *Ad Gentes*, 7
[117] *Ad Gentes*, 11
[118] *General Directory for Catechesis*, 112
[119] *Ad Gentes*, 6
[120] 2 Corinthians 5:1-14; CCC, 851
[121] *Ad Gentes*, 4
[122] CCC, 855
[123] Matthew 5:13-14
[124] *Ad Gentes*, 15
[125] CCC, 856